ENFORCING ETHICS

**A SCENARIO-BASED
WORKBOOK FOR POLICE
AND CORRECTIONS RECRUITS
AND OFFICERS**

DEBBIE J. GOODMAN, M.S.

Prentice Hall
Upper Saddle River, NJ 07458

Library of Congress Cataloging-in-Publication Data

Goodman, Debbie J.

    Enforcing ethics : a scenario-based workbook for police and
corrections recruits and officers / Debbie J. Goodman.

        p.   cm.

    Includes bibliographical references.

    ISBN 0-13-769696-5

    1. Police ethics--Problems, exercises, etc. 2. Correctional
personnel--Professional ethics--Problems, exercises, etc.
I. Title.

HV7924.G66   1998

174' .93632--dc21   97--30114

                                             CIP

Supervising Manager: *Mary Carnis*
Acquisitions Editor: *Neil Marquardt*
Production Editor: *Denise Brown*
Director of Manufacturing and Production: *Bruce Johnson*
Manufacturing Buyer: *Ed O'Dougherty*
Cover Design: *Miguel Ortiz*
Printer/Binder: *Courier Westford*
Marketing Manager: *Frank Mortimer, Jr.*

©1998 by Prentice-Hall, Inc.
A Pearson Education Company
Upper Saddle River, NJ 07458

Printed in the United States of America

10 9 8 7 6 5 4

ISBN 0-13-769696-5

Prentice-Hall International (UK) Limited,London
Prentice-Hall of Australia Pty. Limited, Sydney
Prentice-Hall Canada Inc., Toronto
Prentice-Hall Hispanoamericana, S.A., Mexico
Prentice-Hall of India Private Limited, New Delhi
Prentice-Hall of Japan, Inc., Tokyo
Pearson Education Asia Pte. Ltd., Singapore
Editora Prentice-Hall do Brasil, Ltda., Rio de Janeiro

For Glenn,

my gift, my love, my life

CONTENTS

PREFACE

Some homes look like castles on the outside and cottages on the inside. They appear to be one way but are not, in reality, what they seem to be.

The criminal justice profession is like a castle: prestigious, prominent, and deserving of respect. It is critical that the inhabitants of the castle, *all* officers who have sworn to uphold and enforce the law, conduct themselves in accordance with appropriate standards of behavior.

The profession must be what it is designed to be: equitable, effective, and ethical. Anything less is unacceptable.

Enforcing Ethics has a fundamental purpose: to encourage you, the skilled police or corrections recruit, officer, or supervisor to think critically and carefully about your behavior, your decisions, and your values.

Enforcing Ethics will introduce you to *ethical encounters*: 50 scenarios based upon realistic situations that you may have encountered in the past or situations you may encounter in the future. Also, you will analyze *points to ponder*: 50 questions to discuss among your colleagues. (Any similarity to real cases or people is coincidental.)

Enforcing Ethics will likely lead to opposing points of view, heated discussions, and debates. That's fine. In whatever environment you choose to cover the material, keep one goal in mind: to answer truthfully and openly.

Enjoy *Enforcing Ethics*, and thank you for serving your communities with pride, honesty, and integrity.

ACKNOWLEDGMENTS

To my wonderful family: I love you, Mom, Dad, Corinne, Sam, Sol, Alan, Andy, Bruce, Marisela, Jane, Marion, Mark, Harris, Brooke, Stephen, Christopher, Eddie, Lisa, and Amy.

To the students, faculty, staff, and administrators of Miami-Dade Community College and the School of Justice and Safety Administration: Thank you for your support, Dr. Eduardo Padron, Dr. Jeffrey Lukenbill, Dr. Castell Bryant, Anna Leggett, Ken Glassman, Sam Latimore, Lorren Oliver, Wiley J. Huff, Fred Hutchings, Mike Grimes, Tom Van Buren, Clyde Pfleegor, Miriam Lorenzo, Clark Zen, Ed Preston, Mary Greene, Jean Doubles, and many others.

To the criminal justice professionals who reviewed the workbook: Thank you for your expertise, Chief Curtis Ivy, Chief William Berger, Chief Patrick Kelly, Superintendent Marta Villacorta, Captain Rebecca Tharpe, Officer Bernard Bullock, Vincent J. Petrarca, Brad Farnsworth, Michael T. Charles, Wiley J. Huff, and Dan Durkee.

To Neil Marquardt, Mark Cohen, Denise Brown, and the dedicated staff at Prentice Hall Publishing: Thank you for your efforts on behalf of the workbook.

To Angela Hart: Thank you for your patience and expertise in designing the workbook.

To the men and women of law enforcement and corrections: Thank you for your exceptional service to our communities.

INTRODUCTION

You come home from an emotionally and physically exhausting shift. Today you encountered a suicidal juvenile who listened to your words of encouragement and allowed you to help her. You also apprehended a subject who has been involved in a string of unsolved burglaries. It's fair to say that you put in a "hard day's work." Nice job, Officer! While relaxing at home, you turn on the T.V. set and "channel surf" through the programs. You hear a news reporter announce, "Late this afternoon, officers went to the apartment of Officer Ray Hammond and arrested their fellow colleague for grand theft. Internal affairs investigators claim they have a videotape of Hammond stealing stereo equipment, computers, and cellular phones from local businesses. Officials tell us an in-depth investigation is underway." What did you just hear? An officer who has *sworn* to protect the citizens and enforce the laws has been arrested for *intentionally* violating the law to achieve personal gain? Disgusted by this information, you turn off the television and skim the newspaper. After reading the national news, you turn to the local section of the paper. Your attention becomes drawn to the headline: *Corrections Officers from County Jail Allow Drugs to Enter Facility.* You sit back in your chair, close your eyes, and wonder, "What's going on here?"

What's going on, Officer, is an eye-opening reality check. Unethical behavior has become increasingly prevalent in what many are calling "the morally deficient society" in which we live. When citizens read about or hear about children bringing guns to school, elderly women being brutally raped, and marriages turning bitter and ending in bloodshed, a universal cry for help can be heard in nearly every large city within the

1

United States. To whom do we turn for help? Officers, of course!

Each and every time an officer in any city, county, or state participates in unethical conduct, the entire law enforcement and corrections profession is adversely affected. Clearly, most officers are responsible, dedicated, and ethical. It's unfortunate that *you,* the heroes in the criminal justice field, are not given nearly enough positive attention and recognition, which you rightfully deserve. Officers deserve respect and support; at the same time, citizens deserve peace of mind. One way to give citizens this is to conduct yourself as a *professional* each day for the rest of your career. Whether it's fair or not, whether it's valid or not, people tend to group and judge and categorize others. Often, officers are not viewed individually but collectively. Therefore, if a citizen has had one negative encounter with one officer, chances are the citizen will regard *all* officers in a less-than-favorable manner. Can you afford that? No! So what's an officer to do? Although it is unrealistic to believe that every person walking the planet will regard every officer respectfully, it may be more realistic to believe that every officer "walking the beat" or the "cat walk" can conduct himself or herself in a respectful, professional, and ethical manner. Your conduct leads to how others regard you, treat you, and react to your role. Your role is unlike any other; therefore, your behavior must be sterling or the badge, as well as the profession, may become tarnished. Let's begin our discussion of the study of ethics.

FREE COFFEE, FOOD, AND OTHER STUFF: AN ETHICS DISCUSSION

"Is it O.K. for an officer to accept free coffee, food, and other stuff ?" asked the inquisitive trainee. The answer to this question has been debated for years and will continue to be argued for years to come.

In order to provide an appropriate response to this often-asked question, we need to analyze the definition of the term *ethics*. *Ethics means principles of accepted rules of conduct for a particular individual or group as mandated by law, policy, or procedure.* Let's examine each component of this definition of ethics.

Part 1: Principles of accepted rules of conduct.

Almost everything in life is based upon rules. Sports enthusiasts are familiar with the rules of football. When a player is cited for an "illegal face mask," he has broken an important rule of the game and will incur a penalty. That penalty may adversely impact him as well as his teammates. At the Academy, a trainee who violates an institutional rule may find himself or herself facing counseling, a reprimand, or stringent disciplinary action. At the police or corrections department, an officer who does not adhere to the rules may encounter unwanted media attention, liability, and possibly termination. Therefore, it's fair to say that a significant consequence may act as a deterrent for future inappropriate behavior. However, if no consequence exists or if the consequence is not enforced, the "rule breaker" may be inspired to continue along a path of inappropriate conduct.

Part 2: For a particular individual or group.

Doctors , lawyers, accountants, and officers have something in common. These professionals have strict guidelines they must adhere to in order to maintain their certifications. Professionals of this caliber are held to high standards, and each group member has a unique ethical code to which he or she must comply. Failure to comply may result in decertification.

Part 3: As mandated by law, policy, or procedure.

When something is in writing, we notice it, read it, refer to it, remember it, and ultimately *adhere* to it. Therefore, if criminal justice directors, administrators, trainers, practitioners, and educators are serious about *enforcing ethics*, they must work collaboratively to implement specific state (even federal) guidelines that police and corrections departments must follow. Additionally, department representatives could reinforce these guidelines by writing policies and procedures that explain, clearly and completely, the behaviors that will and will not be tolerated for officers representing their police or corrections departments.

The following illustration easily could be added to a department's standard operating procedures under the ethics category.

The following behaviors are unacceptable and are viewed by this department as unethical:

1. accepting gratuities - gifts, favors, money, or anything given to you for *free*.

2. using unnecessary force - physical abuse, emotional mistreatment, or "roughing-up" suspects in custody.

3. discrimination - mistreating individuals on the basis of race, age, gender, religion, culture, sexual preference, or national origin.

4. lying - in any form, including creating facts to incriminate or protect another.

5. violating laws, rights, or procedures - intentionally making a false arrest, filing a false report, and purposely ignoring departmental procedures.

Add five more unacceptable behaviors to this list.

6.   _____
       _____
       _____
       _____

7.   _____
       _____
       _____
       _____

8. _____
   _____
   _____
   _____

9. _____
   _____
   _____
   _____

10. _____
    _____
    _____
    _____

Remember, if you put it in writing, officers will listen and respond accordingly!

Another point of interest that addresses this discussion is the meaning of the term *gratuity*. *A gratuity is something of value given to another because of that person's status or role. Usually, when a gratuity is offered, the receiver benefits more than the giver.*

An officer should consider the following questions when deciding whether or not a gratuity is being offered:

    1.   Why is this individual offering me this?
    2.   Is this individual offering me this because I am an officer?
    3.   If I were not an officer, would this individual offer me this?
    4.   Ethically, what should I do?

In answering the trainee's question about *free coffee, food, and other stuff,* we can use the four-question approach to reach an appropriate answer.

Question 1: Why is this individual offering me this?
Answer   1: Unless the officer straightforwardly asks the store owner or manager the question of *why,* we can only guess the answer. Maybe the store owner sincerely appreciates your service. Maybe he wants you to be visible in his store to deter would-be perpetrators. Maybe he wants you to fix a ticket he received.

Question 2: Is this individual offering me this because I am an officer?
Answer   2: Yes.

Question 3: If I were not an officer, would this individual offer me this?
Answer   3: No.

Question 4: Ethically, what should I do?
Answer   4: Ethically, you should respectfully decline a citizen's offer of *free* anything. I am not suggesting that the officer who accepts a free cup of coffee is walking the path of corruption and deception. I am suggesting that power and authority are involved here. Officers are powerful people. Some become blinded by this; others do not. Some begin to expect and accept things. Others expect and accept nothing. Remain humble and honest. Expect one thing: the paycheck you earned ethically.

Now that we are on our way to understanding ethics, we need to explore some of the factors that contribute to questionable conduct among police and corrections professionals. At the end of the workbook, we will analyze possible solutions to prevent unethical conduct within the criminal justice field.

Contributing Factors

In order for us to understand what causes an officer to cross the line and behave inappropriately, we need to recognize some of the factors that contribute to *why* an officer may behave a certain way in the first place. The following acronym will pinpoint key areas of this discussion:

> *E* - *Environment*
> *T* - *Training Academy*
> *H* - *Home Life*
> *I* - *Individual Beliefs*
> *C* - *Citizens*
> *S* - *Stress*

Environment

First, the officer's *environment* is going to affect his or her attitudes, beliefs, and actions. Allow me to introduce you to two brothers: Charles and Chris. Both men grew up in a hostile neighborhood. Gangs were prevalent, drug-dealing was common, and violent criminal conduct was a near-everyday occurrence. The brothers' parents worked diligently and legitimately to provide their children with as much as they could afford: a roof over their heads, food in their stomachs, and clothes on their backs. Overall, it wasn't easy, but they managed. As the brothers grew up, their relationship grew apart, as did their interests. Charles went to Penn State and Chris went to the State Penn. Why did one choose education and the other incarceration? Did their environment have something to do with it? Maybe *something* but not *everything*.

Let's meet two officers: Officer George and Officer Allen. Both officers went through the Academy together. They struggled through defensive tactics, legal studies, and report writing. They made it, and now both are sworn officers in different departments. Officer George is on the fast track to the top of the success ladder. He has established an impressive reputation within the department. His colleagues regard him as a *cop's cop*, and the citizens in his patrol neighborhood have written letters of commendation on his behalf. When asked about his work ethic, Officer George responds, "I'm in a great squad. The Sarge is supportive, we know what we need to do, and we do it as a team. I love what I do, and I want to make the department proud." Officer Allen's approach to his position, unfortunately, is quite different from his colleague's. Officer Allen arrives late to work on numerous occasions. He has started drinking alcohol heavily after his shift, and he has had several complaints filed against him for discourteous conduct. When asked about his work ethic, Officer Allen responds, "This department is the worst. We've got tension so thick here, you can cut it with a chainsaw. There's no support, no unity. We've got religious cliques, ethnic issues, and a total lack of caring. The citizens don't help us. They hate us. So what do they expect from me? To be honest, I don't give a sh--!"

What went wrong along the way to distort this picture? We have two young officers who started their careers in law enforcement with enthusiasm and vigor.   Now, one is committed to service and the other is cynical about serving. Is their *working environment* a factor? Yes. It's not an excuse nor is it the only piece to this puzzle. However, the *working environment* in which the officer finds himself or herself will impact his or her desire to succeed and thrive or succumb and falter. Behavior is contagious. When we associate with officers who are upbeat and energetic, we tend to respond to situations in a similar manner. However, when we are in a day-to-day relationship with those who are lethargic and apathetic, we too may find ourselves taking on similar traits. Although we cannot always control our work environment, we can control our actions and reactions at home, on the street, at the department, and at the Academy.

Training Academy

What role does the *Training Academy* play in shaping a recruit's ethics? The Academy plays a tremendous part in how a trainee interacts with fellow colleagues, supervisors, and instructors. One of the most important steps a Training Center can take in encouraging appropriate behavior is to have, in writing, a "Trainee Code of Conduct." The Code should address areas that trainees must remain mindful of on a daily basis while at the Basic Training Academy.

The following example illustrates a sample code which Academies may want to adopt:

We, the administrators, faculty, and staff, of _____ Training Institute, expect trainees at this School to adhere to these standards:

1.   To meet the rigorous academic challenges of this institution.

2.   To communicate respectfully and professionally, at all times, with every person with whom a trainee comes in contact.

3.   To complete assignments and examinations in a timely, honest, and efficient manner. Cheating of any kind is strictly prohibited.

4.   To exhibit pride in being part of a unique learning opportunity.

5.   To remain alert and inquisitive while classroom discussions are taking place.

6.   To arrive promptly for every class session.

7.   To enthusiastically carry out orders given to trainees by staff members.

8.   To seek counsel from the appropriate staff member(s) when matters of a personal nature arise.

9.   To support fellow Academy recruits in their pursuit of excellence.

10.   To report any inappropriate behavior on the part of another trainee, instructor, or officer to the respective command staff.

When individuals are given *clear* and *reasonable* written expectations, more often than not, they comply.

Additionally, Academy instructors play a significant role in shaping and reinforcing the manner in which a trainee interacts with others. Some believe experience is the best teacher. Others say we learn best when we mirror the behavior of professional, well-educated individuals who teach us through their actions. Perhaps it's a combination of both. As we analyze the role of the Academy instructor, whose goal is to teach job-related conduct as well as to encourage ethical ways of *thinking* and *behaving*, many would agree these fine instructors share the following traits:

   * *Professionalism* - Professional instructors take pride in themselves and view the classroom environment as a teaching and learning experience for all. These individuals encourage questions in class, praise effort and achievement, and strive to bring out the best in their students. Professional instructors adhere to a "firm but fair" model. They are aware, at all times, of what they say and the manner in which they say it. They do not use threatening or demeaning tactics. When critique of another's action is warranted, they address the wrongfulness of the act and encourage the trainee to provide solutions, as well as to learn

from the experience. The best Academy instructors are mentors, role models, and people whose conduct should be praised and emulated.

* *Expertise* - Training Centers have an enormous task at hand when it comes to ensuring that all trainees meet the learning objectives consistent with State Certification requirements. Therefore, every instructor must possess a high degree of skill, knowledge, and experience in his or her instructional field. Whether the instructor is a full-time or part-time employee, students recognize those who are knowledgeable from those who pretend to be.

* *Preparation* - Officers are expected to be fully prepared each day for work. They are trained to handle the emotional, physical, and intellectual demands a work shift may bring. Their tools are readily available at all times: handcuffs, notebook, and intellect. The Academy instructor must be prepared to instruct each time he or she enters a classroom. The lesson plan should address the training topic for that day. All handouts must be clearly written and organized. Trainees don't want instructors to "wing it." Students deserve better than that. Do we want officers to "wing it" on the streets or at a corrections facility? No! Preparation is essential.

* *Respect and Courtesy* - If we want trainees to conduct themselves in a respectful manner while at the Academy and in the field, *all* training personnel should show them how it's done by behaving

respectfully and courteously to one another. There are many messages (some subtle and others not) that instructors and staff communicate to the trainees. The training environment must be based upon neutrality. Learning simply cannot take place in an atmosphere that allows discrimination or harassment. Therefore, comments, jokes, or slurs of an inappropriate, offensive nature must be prohibited.

Clearly, the Training Center plays a part in shaping how a criminal justice professional may behave while at the Academy, on the streets, or at the facility. What else affects the manner in which an officer chooses to act?

Home Life

Although the physical structure of some homes may appear similar, what goes on behind closed doors will vary from one household to the next.

When we examine the topic of ethics as it relates to police and corrections officers, we need to take a look at the officer's former and present *home life*.

First, do the parents of officers play a part in shaping how an officer may look at the world and respond to various conditions? Of course, they do! Not every officer was raised in a traditional, two-parent household. Maybe the officer was raised by one parent, a grandparent, or a caring guardian. Whatever the case may be, many children raised in "law enforcement households" respect their parent's profession and choose to follow in similar foot-steps by seeking employment opportunities in the criminal justice field.

14

What if an officer's parents instilled in him or her as a child a lack of tolerance for those who are *different*? Ultimately, this type of early belief system will impact one's thinking as an adult. What if an officer's parents instilled in him or her a healthy respect toward diverse populations? Chances are the officer will grow up interacting well with those who are unique in their own right, as dissimilar as they may appear to be to the officer.

Although the parents of officers are a part of the whole picture, we cannot point accusatory fingers at them. At some point in an officer's young adult life, he or she will start formulating opinions and behaving as he or she *chooses* to behave. Therefore, regardless of what mom or dad or grandpa or guardian once said, officers will make up their own minds about how to behave in different settings and under various circumstances.

Does the officer's present home life affect his or her job-related conduct? Yes, it does! An officer's home life usually fits into one of three categories: living at home with parents, living alone or with a roommate, or living with a spouse. The common thread that weaves its way into an officer's personal life, which affects his or her professional life, is the *emotional support* of a "significant other." For purposes of this discussion, "significant other" refers to a parent, roommate, girlfriend, boyfriend, or spouse. An important question an officer should ask himself or herself is this: *"Does my significant other support my role as an officer?"* If the answer is *yes*, the officer usually experiences peace of mind. If the answer is *no*, interpersonal conflict, at some point, may occur. Clearly, friction at home could lead to ethical concerns on the job.

Another important theme regarding an officer's home life and how it affects the officer's ethics is *loyalty* to one's spouse. Some research studies suggest officers are at risk of experiencing marital problems when compared to other professionals. The following factors have been cited as contributing to the break-up of an officer's marriage:

1. lack of time spent at home
2. secretive demeanor
3. alcohol use
4. adultery
5. consumption with career

Officer, do you want to be happily married? If so, like anything else, it takes hard work, dedication, and a willingness to compromise!

To maintain a loyal, committed, and lasting marriage, officers should consider the following *Ethical Home Rules*:

Rule 1: **Communicate honestly with one another** - When you have had a lousy day and you feel your emotions have been through the wringer, talk it out. Too often, too many spouses of officers find their partners in life "drifting" away from them. Drift is a two-way process. If one starts to drift, the other must pull the partner back to solid, marital ground. Being secretive and keeping your emotions bottled up inside can do more damage than good. Talk it out; don't burn out.

Rule 2:   **Discuss expectations** - Unless an individual is a gifted mind reader, it is virtually impossible to know what one spouse expects from the other until important issues are discussed. What are the financial expectations? Who is expected to help the kids with homework? Who cooks dinner and attends to household duties? Negotiation is the key to understanding and meeting another's reasonable expectations.

Rule 3:   **Wear different hats** - An officer must wear different hats to meet the demands of the profession. One minute you're a psychologist, the next minute a legal scholar, and the next a medical responder. You need to be able to take off your "work hats" and put on your "home hats." Maybe that means being mom or dad; maybe it means being lover or friend; or maybe it means being relaxed with and supportive of those you care about.

Rule 4:   **Work it out** - Every marriage has its bumpy road. For some couples, "for worse" lasts longer than they had hoped. The partners who make it through trying times certainly can appreciate the meaning of togetherness and teamwork. At times, a couple may seek counseling from a skilled, third-party professional. Ultimately, a meaningful marriage is quite similar to an exercise program: With effort, consistency, and a "don't quit" attitude, positive results can be achieved.

17

Rule 5:   **<u>Have fun</u>** - Arrange a dinner or lunch date with
            your spouse.   Plan a weekend get-away
            together. Go roller-blading. Do the things you
            used to do before the pressures of "your status"
            set in.

*List five more things officers should do to make their
relationships positive and lasting.*

Rule 6:   _____
            _____
            _____
            _____

Rule 7:   _____
            _____
            _____
            _____

Rule 8:   _____
            _____
            _____
            _____

Rule 9:   _____
            _____
            _____
            _____

Rule 10:   _____
            _____
            _____
            _____

Individual Beliefs

Another factor influencing an officer's behavior is his or her *individual beliefs.* When an officer treats citizens with respect and dignity, it is because the officer *believes* human beings deserve to be treated with respect and dignity. If an officer treats suspects in an abusive, brutal manner, it is because the officer *believes* this method of treatment is acceptable and justifiable. If an officer crosses the line, it is because he or she *believes* the opportunity exists to do so. Down the road, you may be provoked by an intoxicated subject, an intimidating colleague, or the lure of a quick, easy buck. Officer, be ready to maintain your control and stand for something; otherwise, you risk falling for anything! So, who influences an officer's individual beliefs? Many people contribute to an officer's views of the world around him or her: family members, instructors, friends, supervisors, colleagues, clergy, citizens, and the media. Although others may be influential, an officer *believes* what he or she *chooses* to believe.

It is important for officers to individually and collectively believe in certain fundamental principles. The list of beliefs on page 20 represents universal beliefs of ethical officers.

Officers' Ethical Beliefs

1. As an officer, I believe in the constitutional rights of all people.

2. As an officer, I believe in providing the best service of which I am capable at all times.

3. As an officer, I believe in conducting myself, on and off duty, with pride and professionalism.

4. As an officer, I believe in obeying the laws of the state and the policies of my department.

5. As an officer, I believe in treating people fairly and without favoritism or bias.

Add five more ethical beliefs to this list.

6. As an officer, I believe _____
   _____
   _____
   _____

7. As an officer, I believe _____
   _____
   _____
   _____

8. As an officer, I believe _____
   _____
   _____
   _____

9.   As an officer, I believe _____

_____

_____

_____

10.   As an officer, I believe _____

_____

_____

_____

Citizens

You promised to protect and serve the *citizens* of your community. Unfortunately, some of these men and women may not abide by the laws, and some may not regard favorably what you represent: power, authority, and compliance. Therefore, when an officer finds himself or herself patrolling a neighborhood, day after day, in which negative feelings for law enforcement are pervasive, it's certainly challenging for the officer to view the people in a positive light.

It would be advantageous to the community and the department for administrators to allow their police and corrections colleagues time during a work shift to participate in community-oriented projects.

Let's analyze ways in which police and corrections officers could improve the perception citizens have of them.

1. Officers could attend neighborhood crime watch meetings on a regular basis.

2. Officers could meet with elementary, middle-school, high-school, and college classes to explain the wide range of skills police and corrections officers need to be effective.

3. Officers could volunteer to coach little league games or teach elderly people how to be safe.

4. Officers could get to know the names of residents and local merchants in the community.

5. Officers could prepare meals or collect toys for those who are less fortunate.

What else could officers do to improve their relations with citizens?

6. _____
   _____
   _____
   _____

7. _____
   _____
   _____
   _____

8. _____
   _____
   _____
   _____

9. _____
   _____
   _____
   _____

10. _____
    _____
    _____
    _____

Stress

Thus far, we have discussed various factors that contribute to an officer's decision to behave ethically or unethically. Does stress play a part in how officers conduct themselves?

Absolutely! What is *stress*? *Stress refers to a physical or emotional reaction to a condition or situation.* Perhaps now, more than ever, criminal justice professionals are *stressed out*! Why? Because practically everybody is watching the moves you make: citizens, supervisors, and the media. Therefore, if reactions and behaviors are not managed effectively, officers may find themselves or their colleagues acting inappropriately. Although it is unrealistic to believe that life is, or even should be, completely stress free, it is realistic to examine situations that contribute to stress for officers. Additionally, we will explore warning signs of stress as well as positive measures that can be taken to adapt to difficult conditions. Remember, you can react well to your surroundings, even under adverse situations, and you can conduct yourself ethically.

Experts maintain that the following situations are stressful:

1. Death of a loved one (spouse, family member, close friend)
2. Divorce
3. Termination from employment
4. Serious injury or illness
5. Incarceration in jail or prison
6. Separation from marital partner
7. Financial problems
8. Promotion at work
9. Retirement
10. Marriage
11. Testing
12. Court appearances

What's interesting about this list is that some of the situations are positive (tests, promotion, retirement, and marriage). Therefore, even when good things happen to us, we may still be faced with pressure. What are some of the "signs" officers should look for to determine if they or their colleagues are experiencing stress? The following table illustrates physical and emotional symptoms, ranging from low, medium, high, to severe:

Physical Symptoms		Emotional Symptoms	
Severe	Heart Attack Ulcers	**Severe**	Suicidal thoughts Striking others Frequent outbursts of temper
High	Heart palpitations Vomiting	**High**	Depression Blaming others Feeling angry
Medium	Frequent colds Nervousness Upset stomach	**Medium**	Drinking alcohol to unwind Loss of enthusiasm
Low	Facial tension Headaches	**Low**	Lack of energy Worrying

It is essential for you, police and corrections professionals, to be able to manage your responses and reactions to various conditions, so that you will be effective and healthy representatives of your departments. Experts recommend the following stress-management techniques:

1. breathe deeply
2. exercise regularly
3. eat nutritious foods
4. get enough rest
5. talk about feelings
6. listen to music
7. write about feelings
8. plan for the future
9. laugh a lot
10. participate in enjoyable activities

List five more things you can do to effectively handle stressful situations:

1. _____
   _____
   _____
   _____

2. _____
   _____
   _____
   _____

3. _____
   _____
   _____
   _____

4. _____
   _____
   _____
   _____

5. _____
   _____
   _____
   _____

Now that we have explored six factors which influence an officer's decision to behave ethically or not, it's time for you and your colleagues to read and discuss fifty ethics-related scenarios in the next section titled **Ethical Encounters.** Compare your responses to your colleagues' responses.

ETHICAL ENCOUNTERS

Scenario No. 1

The Club Sandwich

This is your first week on the job as a newly-sworn police officer. You performed well in all of your classes at the Academy. You particularly enjoyed the Ethics class. You found the scenarios interesting, and you made a promise to yourself that you would never accept "freebies" or act in a manner unbecoming to the profession. On this day, you and two senior officers clear a lunch break with the dispatcher. You enjoy a pleasant lunch: a club sandwich. After the meal, your fellow officers get up to leave as you reach for your wallet. One officer asks, "What are you doing?" You respond, "I'm paying for my lunch." He says, "Kid, it's on the house. That's why we eat here." You respond, "At the Academy, we were taught accepting discounted or free meals is unethical." Both officers laugh and say, "Kid, forget the Academy. This is the real world."

Ethically, what should you do? _____

_____

_____

_____

_____

Scenario No. 2

The Perjurer

You and your partner are dispatched to a robbery call. The dispatcher describes the suspect as a white male juvenile, approximately 15-17 years of age, wearing a black T-shirt, blue jeans, and tennis shoes. A few blocks east of the scene, your partner sees someone who fits the suspect's description. Your partner exits the patrol car and shouts, "Police! Stop!" The juvenile starts running, and your partner runs after him. Moments later, your partner fires his revolver, shooting the juvenile in the back. You call fire rescue. They respond and transport the juvenile to the hospital. Meanwhile, your partner takes you aside and says, "I need you to back me. You gotta help me. No matter who asks, tell them it *looked* like the kid was about to draw a weapon." (The truth is, the juvenile did not have a weapon.) Later that day, Officer Thomas from Internal Affairs asks you to tell him what happened.

Ethically, what should you do? _____

_____

_____

_____

_____

_____

Scenario No. 3

The False Report

You and a senior officer are on routine patrol. You come across a juvenile whom you have repeatedly seen in and out of court. You personally know him to have been involved in a total of six property crimes. You are tired of seeing him go through the "revolving door" of justice. Your partner suggests you file a false report on him. After all, the kid's "got to pay" for his actions. Right?

Ethically, what should you do? _____

_____

_____

_____

_____

_____

_____

_____

_____

_____

_____

Scenario No. 4

The Favor

You are a corrections officer who works in a maximum security facility. Yesterday, you misplaced your keys. Fortunately, Inmate Jones found your keys, and he returned them to you. Tonight, he tells you he received a letter from his wife who is filing for divorce. He asks you if he can use the phone to call her. He already used the phone earlier today, and it is now "lights out."

Ethically, what should you do? _____

_____

_____

_____

_____

_____

_____

_____

_____

_____

_____

_____

Scenario No. 5

The Promotional Test

You are studying for the promotional test to become a sergeant. You do not have a lot of time throughout the day to study. A friend of yours, a sergeant, says that he has a "sample copy" of the exam. You know that "sample copies" are forbidden.

Ethically, what should you do? _____

_____

_____

_____

_____

_____

_____

_____

_____

_____

_____

_____

Scenario No. 6

The Money

You are a newly promoted lieutenant in the Narcotics Division of the bureau. While standing at the water fountain, you overhear two of your colleagues, Sergeants Jay Anderson and Dan Foster, discussing last night's $7,500 drug bust. According to the property report, $5,000 was seized. What happened to the $2,500?

Ethically, what should you do? _____

_____

_____

_____

_____

_____

_____

_____

_____

_____

_____

_____

Scenario No. 7

The Cheater

Today you received the results of the sergeant's promotional exam. You devoted a great deal of time to studying. The two officers with the highest score get promoted. You received a score of 94%. Officer Perez received a 95% and Officer Davis received a 96%. You saw Officer Perez refer to hand-written notes during the administration of the test. (Notes are forbidden.) You never told anyone about this.

Ethically, what should you do? _____

_____

_____

_____

_____

_____

_____

_____

_____

_____

_____

_____

Scenario No. 8

The Wallet

You are an off-duty officer who has just completed a three-mile run. You decide to cool off and rest under a big oak tree. You sit down under the tree and see a brown, leather wallet close by. Curiosity gets the best of you, and you open the wallet. Interestingly enough, you find credit cards, identification, and $300 in cash. Nobody else is around.

Ethically, what should you do? _____

_____

_____

_____

_____

_____

What if you found $3,000; $30,000; or more? _____

_____

_____

_____

_____

_____

_____

Scenario No. 9

The Supervisor

You are a newly promoted sergeant appointed to the communications bureau of your department. You supervise six people. During the past several weeks, you have observed "laziness" among five of the six officers: arriving late to work, leaving work early, long personal telephone conversations, and reading the newspaper. The lieutenant has told you to overlook "small stuff" and to give the guys "a break."

Ethically, what should you do? _____

_____

_____

_____

_____

_____

_____

_____

_____

_____

_____

Scenario No. 10

The Harasser

You are a probationary police officer. In two weeks, you will be on permanent status with your department. Your immediate supervisor, Sergeant Richards, repeatedly makes "inappropriate" comments to your colleague, a female probationary police officer regarding her "beautiful face" and "knock-out figure." This morning, you overhear Sergeant Richards tell her, "If you don't go out with me, you'll *never* make it past your probationary stage." She decides to file a report.

Ethically, what should you do? _____

_____

_____

_____

_____

_____

_____

_____

_____

_____

_____

Scenario No. 11

The Whistle Blower

You are a corrections officer who is of high moral character and esteem. Your colleagues and supervisors respect you, and they regard you as a "team player." Today, you overhear two corrections officers discussing their "operation." Apparently, they are allowing inmates to receive narcotics and paraphernalia in the mail. The inmates are paying the officers for "looking the other way."

Ethically, what should you do?_____

_____

_____

_____

_____

_____

_____

_____

_____

_____

Scenario No. 12

The Truth

You are a seventeen-year veteran police officer and you love the work you do. Your nephew just turned 21 years of age. He's as close as a son to you. Throughout his entire life, he listened attentively to your police stories and repeatedly commented, "I want to be just like you when I grow up. I want to be a cop." Now that he's of age, he has started the paperwork process, and he is interviewing with several police departments. The one flaw your nephew has is that he was an "occasional drug user" during adolescence. Despite this, he's a good kid and, in your opinion, would make a fine cop. He asks you if he should mention his past drug usage during upcoming interviews with prospective departments.

Ethically, what should you advise him to do? _____

_____

_____

_____

_____

_____

_____

_____

_____

Scenario No. 13

The Holiday Gift

It's Christmas time, and the citizens in your patrol neighborhood are feeling festive and joyful. Jerry, the owner of Big Jerry's Grill, a well-known diner you frequently eat at, is having a holiday party tonight. Your sergeant tells you to drop by to make sure things are running smoothly. When Jerry sees you, he says, "You know, I really appreciate the work you do. Happy Holidays!" He hands you a crisp $100 dollar bill.

Ethically, what should you do? _____

_____

_____

_____

_____

_____

_____

_____

_____

_____

_____

_____

Scenario No. 14

The Cadet

You are a newly-promoted lieutenant assigned to the Training Bureau of your department. One of the cadets in a basic training class has been reprimanded for the third time for "unprofessional" conduct. According to the Standard Operating Procedures of your department, "Any cadet who receives three reprimands is to be terminated upon notice." This cadet happens to be a well-known politician's son.

Ethically, what should you do? _____

_____

_____

_____

_____

_____

_____

_____

_____

_____

_____

Scenario No. 15

The Aggressor

During a routine patrol with your colleague, Officer Ward, you observe a car traveling 40 mph (10 miles above the posted speed limit). Officer Ward pulls over the car. The driver, a 16-year-old female, produces her driver's license and registration. You hear Officer Ward say, "You stupid *broads* are all the same. If I pull you over again, I'm giving you a ticket." The next day, the driver and her mother meet with your captain, and they file a complaint against Officer Ward for "discourteous conduct." The captain asks you what happened.

Ethically, what should you do? _____

_____

_____

_____

_____

_____

_____

_____

_____

_____

Scenario No. 16

The Brother-In-Law

While on routine patrol, you observe a driver weaving in and out of three lanes of traffic. You notify the dispatcher that you are going to stop the vehicle. When you approach the passenger side of the vehicle, you are surprised to see the driver: your brother-in-law, Rick. Rick's eyes are bloodshot, his speech is slurred, and his breath smells of an unknown alcoholic beverage. When he sees you, he says, "Wow, man, am I glad to see you, and not some other cop."

Ethically, what should you do? _____

_____

_____

_____

_____

_____

_____

_____

_____

_____

_____

Scenario No. 17

The Professional Courtesy Approach

During your morning shift, you observe a motorist traveling 30 mph in a 15 mph school zone. You stop the vehicle, and the motorist immediately identifies himself as a corrections officer from the county. You decide to use "professional courtesy." You do not issue him a ticket.

Is "Professional Courtesy" ethical? _____

_____

_____

_____

_____

_____

_____

_____

_____

_____

_____

_____

Scenario No. 18

The Dinner Break

You and your partner have just cleared a dinner break with the dispatcher. It's been a rough shift: one burglary call in progress and a robbery. You and your partner finally sit down in a comfortable booth. You order a juicy steak dinner from the local barbecue restaurant. Shortly after your order arrives, and you start eating, an elderly woman approaches you and says, "Officer, I locked my keys in my car."

Ethically, what should you do? _____

_____

_____

_____

_____

Will you finish eating, or will you interrupt your meal

to help her? _____

_____

_____

_____

_____

Scenario No. 19

The Crank

It's Halloween! Throughout the day, at the top of each hour, a call comes in to the department regarding a shooting. Each officer who checks the alleged shootings finds them to be untrue. Throughout the day, eleven shooting-related calls have come in. The clock has just struck midnight. A caller reports a shooting and says it's an emergency.

Ethically, what should you do? _____

_____

_____

_____

_____

_____

_____

_____

_____

_____

_____

_____

Scenario No. 20

The Skimmer

Officer Burton, a 22-year veteran of the department, has been assigned to the Narcotics Division for the last eight years. Here and there, he "skims a little off the top." He justifies his behavior by saying, "After 22 years of busting my butt, I'm entitled to more than what they're paying me."

Is Officer Burton's behavior justifiable? _____

_____

_____

_____

_____

_____

_____

_____

_____

_____

_____

_____

_____

Scenario No. 21

The Freebie

For the past several months, you have been stopping by the same convenience store in your patrol area to purchase gum, soda, and potato chips. Last week, a new owner purchased the store. During one of your work breaks, you walk in and the new owner says, "Officer, how nice to see you. Feel free to help yourself to anything you want. You guys do one helluva job."

Ethically, what should you do? _____

_____

_____

_____

_____

_____

_____

_____

_____

_____

_____

Scenario No. 22

The Late Arrival

Your former sergeant was an "easy-going" guy. If you arrived a few minutes late for work, he regarded it as "no big deal." Your newly appointed sergeant, however, is stringent about punctuality. Last week, you arrived twenty minutes late for your morning shift. The sergeant gave you an oral warning stating, "If it happens again, I'll write a disciplinary report." This morning, you find you have approximately ten minutes to get to work. The drive usually takes fifteen minutes. You consider driving your patrol car with the emergency lights on.

Ethically, what should you do? _____

_____

_____

_____

_____

_____

_____

_____

_____

_____

Scenario No. 23

The Time Log

All of the officers in your department are required to submit time logs for off-duty court appearances. Off-duty court appearances equate to "time and a half." It is virtually a common practice for the officers in your squad to give an inflated version of the length of time they spent in court. You are the reporting officer in an armed robbery case. After waiting ten minutes for your case to be called, the clerk announces a continuance.

Ethically, how should you submit your log? _____

_____

_____

_____

_____

_____

_____

_____

_____

_____

_____

Scenario No. 24

The Prostitute

A well-known prostitute on your beat, "Starlight," frantically waves you down as you start the midnight shift. Starlight tells you that her "client," a prominent attorney, beat her and kicked her in the ribs after their "sexual encounter." In addition, she tells you he did not issue her payment for the services she rendered.

Ethically, what should you do? _____

_____

_____

_____

_____

_____

_____

_____

_____

_____

_____

_____

_____

Scenario No. 25

The Cleaners

Tomorrow, your cousin is getting married. On your way to work this morning, you bring your tuxedo to Quick Clean Laundry for dry cleaning and ironing. The laundry closes early today: 2:00 p.m. Your shift ends at 3:00 p.m. You consider stopping by the cleaners while on duty to pick up your tuxedo for the wedding.

Ethically, what should you do? _____

_____

_____

_____

_____

_____

_____

_____

_____

_____

_____

_____

_____

_____

Scenario No. 26

The Movies

You are an off-duty corrections officer. You and your friend decide to see the horror movie playing at the local theater. You happen to be wearing a T-shirt with a badge imprinted on it. The teller at the booth says, "Good evening, Officer. You and your friend can go in without charge."

Ethically, what should you do? _____

_____

_____

_____

_____

_____

_____

_____

_____

_____

_____

_____

_____

Scenario 27

The Joint

You are a corrections officer in a medium-security facility. One of the inmates in your unit, Inmate Monroe, is eligible for parole in two weeks. You favorably regard Inmate Monroe as a "model inmate" and one who complies with the rules. During a cell search, you find a marijuana cigarette underneath Inmate Monroe's mattress.

Ethically, what should you do? _____

_____

_____

_____

_____

_____

_____

_____

_____

_____

_____

_____

Scenario No. 28

The Interrogation

You are the lead investigator in a highly-publicized felony drug-murder case. The defendant, "Big Daddy," has eluded law enforcement for years. Finally, you have enough probable cause and tangible evidence to arrest him. During the interrogation, he is "non-responsive" and answers few of your many questions. After several hours, you and another investigator consult with each other and contemplate a new strategy to get him to talk. Big Daddy's underboss, Leo, may make a deal with the prosecutor to "turn state's evidence" and incriminate Big Daddy. Although Leo has not yet said or agreed to anything, you wonder whether or not you should tell Big Daddy that Leo is the lead witness for the prosecution.

Ethically, what should you do? _____

_____

_____

_____

_____

_____

_____

_____

Scenario No. 29

The Race Card

You are an officer dispatched to the Friendly Food Mart regarding two juveniles who shoplifted beer and potato chips. You are one block away from the store when you see two juveniles who fit the BOLO description. One juvenile is black; the other juvenile is white. You recognize the white juvenile; you arrested him last week for petty theft. The black juvenile does not have a record. You question both kids who tell you they willfully stole the items from the store.

Will you treat both juveniles the same?_____

Ethically, what should you do? _____

_____

_____

_____

_____

_____

_____

_____

_____

Scenario No. 30

The Use of Force Report

You are a corrections officer who has been working at the facility for approximately six weeks. You have heard, through the grapevine, that use of force reports are frowned upon by senior officers and command staff. During your routine patrol of the unit, you observe two inmates wrestling on the ground. You immediately radio for assistance. Officer Nelson arrives, and he orders the inmates to stop fighting. However, they continue fighting. Officer Nelson grabs Inmate Hagerty by the right shoulder and shouts, "That's enough!" Inmate Hagerty raises both arms over his head and says, "Okay, man. Okay." Then Officer Nelson punches Inmate Hagerty in the abdomen and says, "That's to make you think twice the next time." Officer Nelson turns to you and says, "Remember, you didn't see or hear anything."

Ethically, what should you do? _____

_____

_____

_____

_____

_____

_____

Scenario No. 31

The Defense Attorney

You are the reporting officer regarding a first-degree murder case. During courtroom proceedings, the defense attorney questions you and asks, "Officer, did you read my client the Miranda warnings from your card *before* you interrogated him?" In the heat of the moment month's ago, you forgot to read the defendant his rights. As you think about your answer, the defense attorney says, "Well, Officer, we're waiting."

Ethically, what should you do? _____

_____

_____

_____

_____

_____

_____

_____

_____

_____

_____

Scenario No. 32

The Old Man

You have been dispatched to a shoplifting call at Frannie's Pharmacy. When you arrive, the store manager sees you and shouts, "Officer, this man just tried to steal a container of orange juice and a box of laundry detergent. I want him arrested." You ask the man for his identification. He is Abe Lawrence, age 87. You ask him what happened. He tells you that he stole the items because he is on a fixed income and can't afford to purchase the items he needs.

Ethically, what should you do? _____

_____

_____

_____

_____

_____

_____

_____

_____

_____

_____

Scenario No. 33

The "Pissed Off" Officer

You are a rookie officer assigned to a predominantly White, middle-class neighborhood. During the evening shift, you and a senior officer, Officer Houston, are patrolling the neighborhood when he says, "Hey, that kid doesn't *belong* here. Let's question him." You stop your patrol car, get out, and approach him. You ask him for his identification. He gives it to you and says, "Why are you questioning me . . . because I'm black?" Officer Houston frisks and then arrests him. Later that night, Officer Houston says, "That kid just pissed me off with his attitude. I want you to write the report. Charge him with loitering and prowling."

Ethically, what should you do? _____

_____

_____

_____

_____

_____

_____

_____

_____

_____

Scenario No. 34

The Boozer

One of the officers on your squad, Officer Sherwood, has been depressed for the past month. He is in the process of divorcing his wife, who is having an affair with another officer from your department. During a burglary-in-progress call, you radio for back-up. Officer Sherwood arrives ten minutes later. (By this time, you have encountered, subdued, and arrested the subject.) When you approach Officer Sherwood, you notice he has slurred speech, and his breath smells of alcohol. You ask him if he's been drinking. He responds, "Yeah, so what are you going to do about it?"

Ethically, what should you do? _____

_____

_____

_____

_____

_____

_____

_____

_____

Scenario No. 35

The Sleeper

You are a corrections officer assigned to the midnight shift of a maximum-security facility. You and another officer, Officer Adams, are in charge of 80 inmates. Officer Adams likes to take a nap at 2:30 a.m. At approximately 2:45 a.m., two inmates start fighting in C Wing. You radio for back-up. Nobody responds to your post. Fortunately, you are able to quiet the inmates and control the situation.

Ethically, what should you do? _____

_____

_____

_____

_____

_____

_____

_____

_____

_____

_____

_____

Scenario No. 36

The Nose Candy

You and your wife recently purchased a luxury home in an upscale neighborhood. You and your next-door neighbor, Tom, have become pretty good buddies. Tom and his wife invite you and your wife to their house for dinner. While at their home, you open what you believe is a candy jar on the coffee table. However, instead of traditional candy, you see "nose candy," a white, powdery substance which appears to be cocaine. Tom and his wife look at each other, and then he says, "Do you want some?"

Ethically, what should you do? _____

_____

_____

_____

_____

_____

_____

_____

_____

_____

_____

Scenario No. 37

The Aggressive Partner

You and another officer are patrolling the area when you observe a motorist traveling approximately 70 m.p.h. in a 50 m.p.h. zone. You turn on the emergency lights, notify the dispatcher, and follow him. He doesn't pull over right away. After another minute, his left rear tire blows out, and his car slowly comes to a rumbling stop. You and your colleague exit the patrol car. Your colleague says to you, "Back me." He draws his service revolver and shouts, "Get out of the car with your hands up!" The motorist, a juvenile, steps out of the car with his hands up. Your partner orders the juvenile to face the car and to place his hands on the vehicle. The juvenile complies. Then, your colleague starts punching him in the face and ribs. After about three or four punches, your colleague takes out his night stick. You are standing close by and observe every punch and kick. The juvenile does not fight back.

Ethically, what should you do? _____

_____

_____

_____

_____

_____

Scenario No. 38

The Parking Ticket

You and two of your colleagues clear a lunch break with the dispatcher. Before entering Dave's Deli, you notice a car parked in a handicapped zone; the car does not have a disability decal on it. You say to your colleagues, "Guys, I'll be right in. I want to give this joker a ticket." After placing the ticket on the windshield, you enter Dave's Deli, order your usual, and enjoy a pleasant lunch with your fellow officers. When you finish eating, Dave himself comes over and says, "Gentlemen, lunch is on me. By the way, did one of you give me this parking ticket?"

Ethically, what should you do? _____

_____

_____

_____

_____

_____

_____

_____

_____

_____

Scenario No. 39

The Liquor

You are dispatched to a burglary of a liquor store. The owners, a married couple named Joe and Sally Newfeld, provide a detailed account of the cash taken from the register and the liquor the perpetrator(s) stole, as well. The Newfelds seem like nice people. The next day is your day off. You decide to stop by the liquor store to say hello to the Newfelds and to purchase some liquor for tonight's party at your house. The Newfelds thank you for your interest in their well-being. You purchase two bottles of rum and a case of soda. You pay for the items. Mr. Newfeld places a third bottle of rum in the bag and says, "It's just our way of saying thanks."

Ethically, what should you do? _____

_____

_____

_____

_____

_____

_____

_____

_____

Scenario No. 40

The Brunette

You are a male officer who has been married for 12 years. The pretty brunette secretary in your unit has been flirting with you for several weeks. One night, she asks you out for a drink. You meet at a popular bar, share conversation, and order a drink. It's casual. No sexual interactions occur. (You must admit, however, you are attracted to her.) When you arrive home that evening, your wife asks you where you have been.

Ethically, what should you do? _____

_____

_____

_____

_____

_____

_____

_____

_____

_____

_____

Scenario No. 41

The Tune-up

You are an officer who loves motorcycles. Finally, after months of overtime duty, you purchase a great motorcycle. Unfortunately, the bike is in need of a tune-up, so you bring it to Mike's Garage. Mike tells you the bike will be ready in about two hours. Two hours later, you meet Mike in his office, open your wallet, and take out your credit card. Mike sees the badge in your wallet and says, "Why didn't you tell me you're an officer?" He rips up the $65.00 service bill.

Ethically, what should you do? _____

_____

_____

_____

_____

_____

_____

_____

_____

_____

_____

Scenario No. 42

The Friendly Officer

You are a newly-promoted correctional sergeant assigned to the County Jail. You have heard rumors that one of the officers you supervise, Officer John Daniels, has become "friendly" with one of the female inmates, Inmate Lucy Swanson. After dinner this evening, you observe Officer Daniels and Inmate Swanson talking and giggling in the hallway. You see Officer Daniels lean forward, whisper something in Inmate Swanson's ear, and kiss her on the cheek.

Ethically, what should you do? _____

_____

_____

_____

_____

_____

_____

_____

_____

_____

_____

Scenario No. 43

The Stolen Property

This is your first week on the job as a probationary corrections officer. You have been assigned to the property room, where officers collect personal items belonging to the inmates who enter the facility. Today, Corporal Nick Catalano is overseeing the property room. He looks in an envelope containing an inmate's property and says, "This is a nice watch. It's now mine." He puts the watch in his pocket.

Ethically, what should you do? _____

_____

_____

_____

_____

_____

_____

_____

_____

_____

_____

_____

Scenario No. 44

The Instigator

You and another officer, Officer Garcia, are in charge of seventy inmates who are gathered in the yard for recreation. You hear Officer Garcia shout to Inmate Baker, "Hey, boy, get over here! I want to talk to you!" Inmate Baker shouts back, "Don't call me *boy*!" Officer Garcia walks over to Inmate Baker and says, "I'll call you whatever I want to call you!" Inmate Baker pushes Officer Garcia, and the two start fighting. You radio for emergency back-up. Several officers respond, and they are able to control the incident. The shift commander asks you what happened.

Ethically, what should you do? _____

_____

_____

_____

_____

_____

_____

_____

_____

Scenario No. 45

The Tutor

Your son has been having difficulty in school. His teacher gives him a take-home exam. Rudy needs to pass this test; otherwise, he will fail the course. This is his worst subject: Algebra. Algebra was your best subject in school.

Ethically, what should you do? _____

_____

_____

_____

_____

_____

_____

_____

_____

_____

_____

_____

_____

Scenario No. 46

The Wife Beater

You are a police officer who has been dispatched to a domestic violence call. When you arrive, the victim runs out of the house screaming, "Help me! He's going to kill me!" You notice the victim's left cheek is cut, her right eye is swollen, and her dress is torn. You ask her to tell you what happened. She says, "I've had it with his drinking and fooling around! I told him to pack his things and go! That's when he started hitting me!" When you enter the home to question the defendant, you are surprised to see Officer Alexander from your police department. He says, "Thanks for coming out here, but things are cool. I admit I got a little out of hand, but it's under control."

Ethically, what should you do? _____

_____

_____

_____

_____

_____

_____

_____

Scenario No. 47

The Celebrity Inmate

You are a corrections officer and you love baseball. In fact, during your high school days, you were honored with many awards for your athletic achievements on the team. Although you had hopes of playing in the major leagues, a knee injury prevented this from happening. Last week, a well-known baseball player was arrested and booked for narcotics possession. This morning after you conduct a "head count," the inmate takes you aside and whispers, "Officer, if you cut me some slack while I'm here, I'll make sure you get great seats for all the home games. What do you say?"

Ethically, what should you do? _____

_____

_____

_____

_____

_____

_____

_____

_____

Scenario No. 48

The Cuddly Cops

You are a police officer assigned to the midnight shift. Two of your colleagues, Officer Vincent Hall and Officer Jane Torino, are intimately involved with one another. While on duty and in uniform, they go into the property room and "fool around." Meanwhile, you and another officer are the ones handling all of the calls.

Ethically, would should you do? _____

_____

_____

_____

_____

_____

_____

_____

_____

_____

_____

_____

_____

_____

Scenario No. 49

The Fraternity Brother

You are a rookie officer who recently graduated with a Bachelor's degree in Criminal Justice from the local university. Now, you are an officer for the campus police department. Although many of your new friends are police officers, you still keep in touch with your college friends, particularly your fraternity brothers. On this night, you have been dispatched to a reported sexual battery at your former fraternity house. The victim, a 21-year-old female, tells you one of the "frat boys" slipped Rohypnol (Ruffies) into her drink. Then, she states, he raped her. You ask the victim to point out the defendant. She points to Jeff McBride, a friend of yours. You ask him to tell you what happened. He says, "She seemed really tense, so I put a Ruffie in her drink to relax her. Yeah, we had sex, but she consented."

Ethically, what should you do? _____

_____

_____

_____

_____

_____

_____

Scenario No. 50

The Jokers

You are a corrections officer in a minimum security facility. Your squad is comprised of four male officers and one female officer. Some of the male officers believe that a woman's place is *not* as a corrections officer. On this day, three of the officers (not including you) decide to cut out pictures of naked women from a magazine. They write comments on the pictures such as "this could be you" and "pursue your life's work." The officers leave these pictures in her locker. When the female officer finds the pictures, she immediately notifies the sergeant. The sergeant asks all of the officers in the squad if they know anything about the incident. Each of your colleagues says "no."

Ethically, what should you do? _____

_____

_____

_____

_____

_____

_____

_____

POINTS TO PONDER AND DISCUSS

Respond in detail to each question. As you do, try to think about the struggles you may encounter.

1. What is your definition of an ethical officer?

   _____

   _____

   _____

   _____

2. What is your definition of an unethical officer?

   _____

   _____

   _____

   _____

3. Do you believe an officer who accepts a free cup of coffee or a discounted meal is acting appropriately or inappropriately?

   _____

   _____

   _____

   _____

4. If a "good" officer performs a "bad" act, does that make him or her ethical or unethical? Why?

   _____

   _____

   _____

   _____

5. If a "bad" officer performs a "good" act, does that make him or her ethical or unethical? Why?

_____

_____

_____

_____

6. Why did you decide to enter the criminal justice profession?

_____

_____

_____

_____

7. Do you think the general public views officers as primarily ethical or unethical?

_____

_____

_____

_____

8. Do you view the general public as primarily ethical or unethical?

_____

_____

_____

_____

9. Is the public's perception of you as an officer important?

_____

_____

_____

_____

10. Are most of your friends affiliated with the criminal justice field?

_____

_____

_____

_____

11. Is it important for you to "fit in" with your fellow officers?

_____

_____

_____

_____

12. Do you believe it is ever necessary for you to compromise your personal values in order to be part of the team?

_____

_____

_____

_____

13 Do you believe that individuals in command positions have achieved their status ethically or unethically?

_____

_____

_____

_____

14. Do you believe that undercover investigations and operations are ethical?

_____

_____

_____

_____

15. Do you feel "a part of" or "apart from" the community in which you work?

_____

_____

_____

_____

16. Do you feel "a part of" or "apart from" the department for which you work?

_____

_____

_____

_____

17. Do you feel "a part of" or "apart from" your family?

_____

_____

_____

_____

18. Do you feel you have changed in any way(s) since becoming a recruit or officer?

_____

_____

_____

_____

19. If you have changed, do you regard these changes as mainly positive or negative?

_____

_____

_____

_____

20. To whom are you most loyal?

Yourself	_____	Your community	_____
Your family	_____	Your friends	_____
Your department	_____	Your religion	_____

21. Do you feel you are more likely to give in to or stand up to pressure from your colleagues?

_____

_____

_____

_____

22. What pressures are you most likely to give in to?

Political	_____	Family	_____
Departmental	_____	Friends	_____
Media	_____	Other	_____

23. Would you follow a direct order from a supervisor if you believed the order was unethical or inappropriate?

_____

_____

_____

_____

24. Have you ever done something within the scope of your employment that you believe is unethical?

_____

_____

_____

_____

25. Are you able to separate your professional life from your personal life?

_____

_____

_____

_____

26. Should supervisors be held accountable for the unethical actions of their subordinates?

_____

_____

_____

_____

27. Do you think "whistle-blowers" protect the public interest?

_____

_____

_____

_____

28. Do you think "whistle-blowers" help or hurt the department?

_____

_____

_____

_____

29. As an officer, when is it O.K. to look the other way?

_____

_____

_____

_____

30. As an officer, when is it O.K. to file a false report?

_____

_____

_____

_____

31. As an officer, when is it O.K. to be aggressive?

_____

_____

_____

_____

32. If a man steals a loaf of bread because he is starving, is his behavior ethical or unethical?

_____

_____

_____

_____

33. If a juvenile steals a pack of cigarettes to impress his friends, is his behavior ethical or unethical?

_____

_____

_____

_____

34. Does the act itself determine whether or not a behavior is ethical, or is it the individual's *intent* that determines ethics?

_____

_____

_____

_____

35. Are your official decisions ever influenced by another's race, age, gender, social status, or attitude?

_____

_____

_____

_____

36. If you knew that a fellow officer participated in unethical conduct, what, if anything, would you do about it?

_____
_____
_____
_____

37. Do you believe other officers are primarily ethical or unethical?

_____
_____
_____
_____

38. If officers were paid higher salaries, would there be fewer instances of unethical conduct?

_____
_____
_____
_____

39. Is it ethical for departments to conduct routine drug tests of their employees?

_____
_____
_____
_____

40. Do you believe that all officers must stick together regardless of the circumstances?

_____
_____
_____
_____

41. What is your definition of "professionalism"?

_____
_____
_____
_____

42. What is your definition of "gratuity"?

_____
_____
_____
_____

43. What is your definition of "crossing the line"?

_____
_____
_____
_____

44. Do you believe an officer should adopt an "us vs. them" philosophy?

_____
_____
_____
_____

45. As an officer, what goals have you set for yourself?

_____
_____
_____
_____

46. What is the most unethical thing a police or corrections officer could do?

_____
_____
_____
_____

47. Would you have difficulty arresting someone you know (friend, neighbor, fellow officer, or family member)?

_____
_____
_____
_____

48. Why do you think some officers behave unethically and inappropriately?

_____
_____
_____
_____

49. How do you view your present work environment? Is it generally supportive or non-supportive?

_____

_____

_____

_____

50. Do you believe one officer can make a difference?

_____

_____

_____

_____

WHERE DO WE GO FROM HERE?

Are we able to rise above the O.J. Simpson case and the role Detective Mark Fuhrman played in it? Have we fully recovered from the graphic images of officers beating Rodney King while he was handcuffed on the pavement? It's difficult to say how citizens will perceive officers in the future if their memories remain focused on these disturbing, isolated findings. If there is any way to gain citizens' trust of and respect for criminal justice personnel, it is through the continuous heroic actions taking place every day. The hundreds and thousands of men and women who so selflessly give of their time, their hearts, and their lives to make the streets safer for all of us should be *commended*. Although their stories of courage and sacrifice may not make headlines, we know that they represent the majority of police and corrections officers.

Early on in the workbook, we discussed six factors that influence an officer's decision to behave ethically or not. Let's review these points.

First, an officer's *environment* refers to external influences: choices and behaviors of family members and peers, as well as exposure to appropriate and inappropriate activities. An officer's *work environment* refers to how the officer perceives the role as well as those with whom he or she works.

Second, the *training academy* plays a part in how recruits interact with others and how instructors present the role of a criminal justice representative.

Third, the officer's *home life* refers to views parents may have instilled during formative years, as well as support the officer receives from significant others.

Fourth, every officer has his or her *individual beliefs* about others and behaviors that they view as acceptable or not for the profession.

Fifth, *citizens* affect an officer's decision-making ability by their conduct and demeanor toward the officer.

Finally, *stress* must be managed effectively so the officer can be emotionally, physically, and intellectually fit for the rigorous duties he or she is called upon to perform.

At this time, we will address measures criminal justice administrators can take to encourage ethical conduct among police and corrections professionals.

WAYS TO ENFORCE ETHICS

1. Identify in writing, within department policy and/or procedures, the specific *behaviors* that are unacceptable.

2. Identify in writing, within department policy and/or procedures, the specific *consequences* of inappropriate behaviors.

3. Implement "Ethics" training seminars for all sworn and civilian personnel.

4. Conduct routine drug tests of all employees.

5. Reinforce positive behavior by rewarding ethical actions.

6. Encourage officers to report unethical behavior of fellow colleagues.

7. Hold employees and supervisors accountable for their actions and inactions.

8. Ask employees for their recommendations regarding ways to encourage an ethical work force.

9. Create a working environment based upon pride, praise, and professionalism.

10. Lead by example each and every day.

Also, professional police and corrections departments should have, in writing, a *value statement*. *A value statement represents the principles that officers and administrators regard as essential to the effective functioning of their department.* Here are two examples of value statements:

Police Value Statement

We, the officers of _____
Police Department, are committed to enforcing the laws, protecting the citizens, and preserving the peace. The following represents the values which we view as most important to our ethical, professional police department:

Value 1:   We will uphold the rights of all citizens regardless of race, color, creed, gender, culture, or religion.

Value 2:   We will conduct ourselves, at all times, with integrity, pride, and professionalism.

Value 3:   We will provide the best service possible to the citizens we have sworn to protect.

Value 4:   We will view crime prevention as the fundamental responsibility of our ethical, professional police department.

Value 5:   We will vigorously pursue those who commit criminal acts and those who threaten the safety and well-being of our citizens.

Create five more police value statements.

Value 6:   We will _____
_____
_____
_____

Value 7:   We will _____
_____
_____
_____

Value 8:   We will _____
_____
_____
_____

Value 9:   We will _____
_____
_____
_____

Value 10:   We will _____
_____
_____
_____

In order for the value statement to motivate representatives of the police department, roll-call supervisors should ask a police officer, at least once a week, to read aloud the value statement at the closure of a meeting.

Corrections Value Statement

We, the officers of _____
Corrections Department, are committed to ensuring the care, custody, and control of the offender population we serve. The following represents the values which we view as most important to our ethical, professional corrections department:

Value 1:   We will treat fairly all offenders regardless of race, color, creed, gender, culture, or religion.

Value 2:   We will conduct ourselves, at all times, with integrity, pride, and professionalism.

Value 3:   We will strive to work as a team in meeting the day-to-day challenges of our institution.

Value 4:   We will work cooperatively with public safety agencies to enhance the effectiveness of our department.

Value 5:   We will provide an environment that is safe and secure for offenders and staff.

Create five more corrections value statements.

Value 6:   We will _____

_____

_____

_____

Value 7:   We will _____

_____

_____

_____

Value 8:   We will _____

_____

_____

_____

Value 9:   We will _____

_____

_____

_____

Value 10:   We will _____

_____

_____

_____

Again, to maximize the impact of the value statement, supervisors should ask a corrections officer, at least once a week, to read aloud the value statement at the closure of a meeting.

What else can be done to encourage ethical representation? Recruits and officers need to be mindful of the various situations they may encounter and what they should and should not do. We'll call this list "Three Do's and a Don't."

I.   <u>Court</u>

1.   Do come prepared with the facts of a case.
2.   Do respond politely to a defense attorney's questions.
3.   Do tell the truth at all times.

Don't lose control during cross examination.

II.   <u>Training Academy</u>

1.   Do interact with trainees, staff, instructors, and supervisors in a respectful manner.
2.   Do your best to learn all lessons being taught.
3.   Do support your colleagues in their pursuit of success.

Don't violate Academy policies or procedures.

III.   <u>Gifts and Favoritism</u>

1.   Do decline offers of *free* anything.
2.   Do treat individuals without favoritism or bias.
3.   Do remember the code you promised to uphold.

Don't bend the rules; once something bends, it could become broken.

IV. Citizens

1. Do provide the citizens of your community with your best service.
2. Do communicate courteously during vehicle stops and ticketing.
3. Do attend neighborhood crime watch meetings.

Don't lose your temper, even if a citizen loses his or her cool.

V. Private Life

1. Do think intelligently about how you conduct your private life.
2. Do choose friends who are law-abiding individuals.
3. Do effectively communicate your feelings with significant others.

Don't do anything to shame your family or your department.

VI. Facility

1. Do adopt a "firm but fair " philosophy with inmates.
2. Do cooperate with other officers and supervisors.

3.   Do adhere to your department's rules and regulations.

Don't allow yourself to become manipulated by offenders.

VII.   <u>Decision-Making</u>

1.   Do think about what you were trained to do.
2.   Do consider the consequences associated with unethical conduct.
3.   Do what you took an oath to do.

Don't engage in any unfavorable conduct, on or off duty.

Finally, when you make a decision to behave a certain way, ask yourself this question:

"WOULD I FEEL COMFORTABLE HAVING MY BEHAVIOR TELEVISED ON THE LOCAL OR NATIONAL NEWS?"

You never know.

ANSWER GUIDE TO SCENARIOS

Note: It is the opinion of the author that the answers provided for the scenarios are consistent with ethical guidelines in most states. If your responses differ, discuss why among your colleagues.

Scenario No. 1

The Club Sandwich

You should tell your fellow officers that you feel comfortable paying for your own lunch and that you plan to do so for the rest of your career!

Scenario No. 2

The Perjurer

Lying to protect another officer's mistake is a quick way to end an ethical career. Remember: One lie leads to many more. Telling the truth about an incident may be a bit of a stumble, but a stumble prevents a fall! Is lying worth falling for? No!

Scenario No. 3

The False Report

Wrong! The kid does not have to pay for his actions when he has not committed a violation of law. Creating facts to incriminate another is dishonest.

Scenario No. 4

The Favor

If you allow Inmate Jones to use the phone, you are rewarding his honesty. However, showing favoritism toward an inmate could lead to manipulation. Consult with your supervisor.

Scenario No. 5

The Promotional Test

You should study the material that you were told to study and decline your friend's offer to examine a sample copy of the test.

Scenario No. 6

The Money

As an individual in a supervisory position, you are called upon to oversee the actions of other personnel. Therefore, you should question Sergeants Anderson and Foster about the money. Inform Internal Affairs about the matter if their answer does not explain the situation.

Scenario No. 7

The Cheater

You should have reported this incident right away. However, you are still obligated to file an anonymous complaint so he will be questioned by Internal Affairs.

Scenario No. 8

The Wallet

You should contact the owner and return the wallet, credit cards, identification, and *cash* (regardless of the amount!).

Scenario No. 9

The Supervisor

Have a meeting to advise them of what behaviors are acceptable and unacceptable. Then, deal with each subsequent violation as it arises.

Scenario No. 10

The Harasser

When asked, attach an addendum to her report stating *specifically* what you heard Sergeant Richards say to her. Remember: Stand for something!

Scenario No. 11

The Whistle Blower

Most police and corrections officers fear being regarded as a "snitch" or "rat." However, failing to report a violation of law or policy when you have knowledge of a wrongful act could make you liable as well. You should inform your supervisor of the conversation you heard.

Scenario No. 12

The Truth

You should advise your nephew to tell the truth. Nothing can change the fact that your nephew used drugs as an adolescent. He should mention his involvement and start his career in law enforcement, honestly!

Scenario No. 13

The Holiday Gift

You should thank Jerry for his appreciation of your service and decline the $100 dollar bill.

Scenario No. 14

The Cadet

Favoritism is a form of unethical conduct. The cadet, whether a well-known politician's son or not, received three reprimands. He should be punished according to departmental policy.

Scenario No. 15

The Aggressor

Tell the captain what happened. You did nothing wrong; Officer Ward did.

Scenario No. 16

The Brother-In-Law

You have one option: Arrest him.

Scenario No. 17

The Professional Courtesy Approach

The concept of "professional courtesy" is debatable. Does it mean you will overlook *all* inappropriate practices of a fellow officer? Will you overlook *some* things and not others? Is this favoritism? If so, the *code of ethics* states "enforce the law without favor." If you have used your discretion and allowed other speeders to go with only a warning, you are treating him without favor.

Scenario No. 18

The Dinner Break

You are a public servant. You should help the woman retrieve her keys from the vehicle before you finish your meal, unless department policy prohibits you from assisting in this situation. Some departments have adopted such a policy because these calls keep them from their law enforcement duties.

Scenario No. 19

The Crank

It does not matter how many "crank calls" have come in. It is an officer's responsibility to investigate a shooting-related call. Investigate!

Scenario No. 20

The Skimmer

Officer Burton's behavior is not justifiable! He's stealing; therefore, the appropriate disciplinary action must be taken.

Scenario No. 21

The Freebie

You should thank the new owner of the convenience store for his appreciation of your service. Respectfully decline his offer to accept free gum, soda, and potato chips. Continue to pay for your items.

Scenario No. 22

The Late Arrival

Misusing your patrol vehicle and using the emergency lights in a non-emergency situation is neither prudent nor appropriate and may expose you to civil liability should the misuse result in an accident.

Scenario No. 23

The Time Log

Although some officers submit "inflated" versions of the time they spent in court, the ethical officer should submit a time log that accurately reflects the actual time he or she spent in court. Check your department policy.

Scenario No. 24

The Prostitute

The victim in this scenario may appear to lack credibility because she is a prostitute. However, she alleges she incurred a beating, and you should gather the facts and write an incident report. If you have other evidence, you should also arrest her for prostitution since she just admitted the crime to you.

Scenario No. 25

The Cleaners

Check your department policy regarding this matter. Typically, you should pick up your tuxedo on your *personal* time; you should not pick up your tuxedo while on duty.

Scenario No. 26

The Movies

You should thank the teller for the offer of free movie tickets, and tell him or her that you will pay for your own movie ticket.

Scenario No. 27

The Joint

As a corrections officer, you are responsible for ensuring the care, custody, and control of inmates. You are not called upon to overlook violations of facility policy. Therefore, because you found a marijuana cigarette during a cell search, you should confiscate the contraband, question Inmate Monroe, and write a report.

Scenario No. 28

The Interrogation

Check State and Federal statutes regarding lawful procedures for the questioning of defendants.

Scenario No. 29

The Race Card

Race is irrelevant. In this case, you have enough probable cause to arrest both juveniles, and you should arrest them for the crime they committed.

Scenario No. 30

The Use of Force Report

All officers know excessive force is unethical and inappropriate. You witnessed Officer Nelson using excessive force on Inmate Hagerty; therefore, you should inform the supervisor of the unit of the incident.

Scenario No. 31

The Defense Attorney

When officers testify in court, they *swear* to tell the truth. You should respond honestly to the defense attorney's question. After this experience, you will never again forget to read Miranda warnings to a subject!

Scenario No. 32

The Old Man

Mr. Lawrence committed a crime: petty theft. The manager wants him arrested, and Mr. Lawrence admits to stealing the items; therefore, you should arrest him.

Scenario No. 33

The "Pissed Off" Officer

This scenario represents a turning point in a rookie officer's career. A senior officer asks you to write a false report, based upon a false charge, which led to a false arrest. He made the arrest, so he should file the report, not you. Inform your supervisor of the incident.

Scenario No. 34

The Boozer

What are you going to do about it? You observe a fellow officer, while he is on duty, in an intoxicated state. You should notify your supervisor *immediately* before the officer or someone else gets hurt.

Scenario No. 35

The Sleeper

First, question Officer Adams to ensure he was sleeping. Then, you should inform the shift commander of the incident.

Scenario No. 36

The Nose Candy

If the incident occurs within your jurisdiction, make an arrest! If it is outside your jurisdiction, notify local authorities. This is a felony! You are required to take action.

Scenario No. 37

The Aggressive Partner

You should intervene and stop your partner from abusing the juvenile. In addition, you should notify your supervisor of the incident.

Scenario No. 38

The Parking Ticket

You should explain to Dave that a vehicle without a disability decal and parked in a handicapped zone warrants a ticket. Pay for your own lunch.

Scenario No. 39

The Liquor

You should thank Mr. Newfeld for offering you a bottle of liquor and respectfully decline his gift.

Scenario No. 40

The Brunette

As discussed earlier, ethics in the home is as *important* as ethics in the work place; therefore, tell your wife where you've been. (If she gets mad at you, don't go out with the secretary.)

Scenario No. 41

The Tune-up

You should tell Mike to prepare another bill because you will pay for the service provided.

Scenario No. 42

The Friendly Officer

You should tell Officer Daniels his behavior is unacceptable and inappropriate. Write a report about the incident, and seek the appropriate disciplinary action.

Scenario No. 43

The Stolen Property

You should inform the supervisor about the incident and write a report.

Scenario No. 44

The Instigator

You should tell the shift commander what Officer Garcia said, and which instigated the confrontation.

Scenario No. 45

The Tutor

You should encourage Rudy to put forth his best effort. You can offer him guidance and support; however, you should not take the exam for him.

Scenario No. 46

The Wife Beater

You have enough probable cause to make an arrest, and that's what you should do. Arrest him.

Scenario No. 47

The Celebrity Inmate

Celebrity or not, you are supposed to treat inmates fairly and without favoritism. Let him know that's what you're planning to do. Decline his offer of baseball tickets.

Scenario No. 48

The Cuddly Cops

Inform your immediate supervisor about the officers' unethical behavior.

Scenario No. 49

The Fraternity Brother

Although fraternity brothers pledge their loyalty to one another, you have pledged your loyalty to the citizens, to your department, and to the state! Arrest him.

Scenario No. 50

The Jokers

This is not a joke! This is sexual harassment, and it must not be tolerated anytime or anywhere! Tell the sergeant what you know.

APPENDIX

LAW ENFORCEMENT CODE OF ETHICS

As a Law Enforcement Officer, my fundamental duty is to serve mankind; to safeguard lives and property; to protect the innocent against deception, the weak against oppression or intimidation, and the peaceful against violence or disorder; and to respect the Constitutional rights of all men to liberty, equality, and justice.

I will keep my private life unsullied as an example to all; maintain courageous calm in the face of danger, scorn, or ridicule; develop self-restraint; and be constantly mindful of the welfare of others. Honest in thought and deed in both my personal and official life, I will be exemplary in obeying the laws of the land and the regulations of my department. Whatever I see or hear of a confidential nature or that is confided to me in my official capacity will be kept ever secret, unless revelation is necessary in the performance of my duty.

I will never act officiously or permit personal feelings, prejudices, animosities, or friendships to influence my decisions. With no compromise for crime and with relentless prosecution of criminals, I will enforce the law courteously and appropriately without fear or favor, malice or ill will, never employing unnecessary force or violence, and never accepting gratuities.

I recognize the badge of my office as a symbol of public faith, and I accept it as a public trust to be held so long as I am true to the ethics of the police service. I will constantly strive to achieve these objectives and ideals, dedicating myself before God to my chosen profession . . . law enforcement.

(Reprinted with permission from the International Association of Chiefs of Police.)

AMERICAN CORRECTIONAL ASSOCIATION CODE OF ETHICS

Preamble

The American Correctional Association expects of its members unfailing honesty, respect for the dignity and individuality of human beings, and a commitment to professional and compassionate service. To this end, we subscribe to the following principles:

1. Members shall respect and protect the civil and legal rights of all individuals.

2. Members shall treat every professional situation with concern for the welfare of the individuals involved and with no intent to personal gain.

3. Members shall maintain relationships with colleagues to promote mutual respect within the profession and improve the quality of service.

4. Members shall make public criticisms of their colleagues or their agencies only when warranted, verifiable, and constructive.

5. Members shall respect the importance of all disciplines within the criminal justice system and work to improve cooperation with each segment.

6. Members shall honor the public's right to information and share information with the public to the extent permitted by law subject to individuals' right to privacy.

7. Members shall respect and protect the right of the public to be safeguarded from criminal activity.

8. Members shall refrain from using their positions to secure personal privileges or advantages.

9. Members shall refrain from allowing personal interest to impair objectivity in the performance of duty while acting in an official capacity.

10. Members shall refrain from entering into any formal or informal activity or agreement which presents a conflict of interest or is inconsistent with the conscientious performance of duties.

11. Members shall refrain from accepting any gifts, service, or favor that is or appears to be improper or implies an obligation inconsistent with the free and objective exercise of professional duties.

12. Members shall clearly differentiate between personal views/statements and views/statements/positions made on behalf of the agency or the Association.

13. Members shall report to appropriate authorities any corrupt or unethical behaviors in which there is sufficient evidence to justify review.

14. Members shall refrain from discriminating against any individual because of race, gender, creed, national origin, religious affiliation, age, or any other type of prohibited discrimination.

15. Members shall preserve the integrity of private information; they shall refrain from seeking information on individuals beyond that which is necessary to implement responsibilities, and perform their duties; members shall refrain from revealing nonpublic data unless expressly authorized to do so.

16. Members shall make appointments, promotions, and dismissals in accordance with established civil service rules, applicable contract agreements, and individual merit, rather than furtherance of personal interests.

17. Members shall respect, promote, and contribute to a work place that is safe, healthy, and free of harassment in any form.

Adopted August 1975 at the 105th Congress of Correction
Revised August 1990 at the 120th Congress of Correction
Revised August 1994 at the 124th Congress of Correction

BIBLIOGRAPHY

The following resources are recommended for further reading:

Close, Daryl, and Meier, Nicholas. *Morality in Criminal Justice: An Introduction to Ethics.* California: Wadsworth Publishing Co., 1995.

Elliston, Frederick, and Feldberg, Michael. *Moral Issues in Police Work.* New Jersey: Rowan and Allanheid, 1985.

Facione, Peter; Scherer, Donald; and Attig, Thomas. *Ethics and Society* (Second Edition) New Jersey: Prentice Hall, 1991.

Florida Department of Law Enforcement. *Basic Recruit Training Program for Police and Corrections.* 1993.

Fried, Charles. *Right and Wrong.* Massachusetts: Howard University Press, 1978.

Goldstein, Herman. *Police Corruption.* District of Columbia: Police Foundation, 1975.

Hansen, Paul. *Creative Stress Management for Law Enforcement and Corrections.* Colorado: Creative Stress Management, Ltd., 1981.

Mappes, Thomas and Zembaty, Jane. *Social Ethics: Morality and Social Policy.* New York: McGraw-Hill, Inc., 1977.

Pollock, Joycelyn. *Ethics in Crime and Justice: Dilemmas and Decisions* (Second Edition). California: Wadsworth Publishing Co., 1994.

Ruchelman, Leonard. *Who Rules the Police?* New York: New York University Press, 1973.

Stinchcomb, Jeanne. *Managing Stress: Performing Under Pressure.* Maryland: American Correctional Association, 1995.